"SUCCESS AND ITS ENEMY CALLED CRISIS"

BY

PASTOR TASHA TAYLOR

B.A.C.E.

TABLE OF CONTENTS

Unless otherwise noted, all scripture references are from the King James Version (KJV)

PRIMARY SOURCE OUTLINE

Book- A Guide to Crisis Intervention

Author- Kristi Kanel

A. Understanding a need for Counsel
1. Contacting a Pastor
2. Contacting Secular advice
3. Contacting Medical Professionals

B. Ideas of Kristi Kanel concerning learning, memory and cognition
1. The Call for Help
2. Gerald Caplan's "Seven Characteristics of Effective Coping Behavior"
3. Ideas on Cognition with Kanel

C. Ideas of Clyde Narramore concerning learning, memory and cognition
1. What Activates Successful Thinking
2. Important Pointers for Counselors

D. Ideas of Richard Olson concerning learning, memory and cognition

1. It is Safe to Ask

E. Ideas of Wayne Oates concerning learning, memory and cognition
1. Help for Personality Disorders in the Church

F. Ideas of Dr. William Backus concerning learning, memory and cognition
1. What Qualifies to Counsel
   G. Pre-Birth Experience

   H. Childhood

   l. Adolescence and College Students

   J. Adulthood

   K. Elder hood

   L. Conclusion

"Glossary"

1. **Learning** - the acquisition of knowledge or skills through experience, study, or by being taught.[1]

2. **Cognition** - the mental action or process of acquiring knowledge and understanding through thought, experience, and the senses.[2]

3. **Memory** - 1. The faculty by which the mind stores and remembers information: "I've a great memory for faces" 2. Something remembered from the past; a recollection: "one of my earliest memories is of sitting on his knee" synonyms: recollection · remembrance · reminiscence · impression 3. The part of a computer in which data or program instructions can be stored for retrieval.[3]

[1] Oxford Dictionaries, s.v. "learning," accessed November 1, 2015, http://www.oxforddictionaries.com/us/

[2] Oxford Dictionaries, s.v. "cognition," accessed November 1, 2015, http://www.oxforddictionaries.com/us/

[3] Oxford Dictionaries, s.v. "memory," accessed November 1, 2015, http://www.oxforddictionaries.com/us/

4. **Failure** - 1. lack of success: "an economic policy that is doomed to failure" · synonyms: lack of success · non-fulfillment · defeat · collapse · 2. the omission of expected or required action: "their failure to comply with the basic rules" synonyms: negligence · dereliction · omission · oversight 3. the action or state of not functioning: "symptoms of heart failure."[4]

5. **Success**- Attainment of higher social status. Achievement of a goal, for example academic success. The opposite of failure.[5]

6. Crisis- A time of intense difficulty, trouble, or danger.[6]

---

[4] Oxford Dictionaries, s.v. "failure," accessed November 1, 2015, http://www.oxforddictionaries.com/us/

[5] Wikipedia, s.v. "success," accessed November 1, 2015, https://en.wikipedia.org/wiki/Success

[6] http://www.oxforddictionaries.com/us/definition/american_english/crisis

"Introduction"

The research material in this paper might be able to uplift the hearts of many readers one day because, it focuses on an area that affects all people in their human life, crises. When an individual is in need or dependent upon another individual it might be looked down upon in our society; unless, it is to aid children or the elderly. However, there are reports of elder abuse and child abuse; because, patience and love is lacking in our world today. Thank God for the few gifted or compassionate people who give to help those in need. Yet, many people undergoing crisis often feel a sense of worthlessness, because they might not be able provide to meet their own basic needs. Society tends to makes people feel that in adulthood they should have all the right answers, and make all the right choices or they are deemed a failure or infidel; however, crisis happens to all people at one point or another in every life. Crisis can occur from a divorce, death, theft, infidelity or some other life changing event. These events can be avoided, but not everyone is absolutely perfect that they just seem to jump over every crisis life throws at them. A prayer filled life, however can help people to avoid the very death traps of the enemy. In Psalms 91 the Bible talks about being in the secret place of the Most High. It asserts believers that by being in a place of prayer, which is the "secret place" one can attain protection from God. Psalms 91 says:

Whoever dwells in the shelter of the Most High will

rest in the shadow of the Almighty. I will say of

the Lord, "He is my refuge and my fortress, my

God, in whom I trust." **Surely he will save you from**

the fowler's snare and from the deadly pestilence.

He will cover you with his feathers, and under his

wings you will find refuge; his faithfulness will be

your shield and rampart. You will not fear the

terror of night or the arrow that flies by day,

nor the pestilence that stalks in the darkness,

nor the plague that destroys at midday. A

thousand may fall at your side, ten thousand

at your right hand, but it will not come near

you. You will only observe with your eyes and

see the punishment of the wicked. If you say,

"The Lord is my refuge, and you make the Most

High your dwelling, **no harm will overtake you,**

no disaster will come near your tent.

The Bible goes on further to express that God will also send His angels to protect those who dwell in that "secret place" called prayer. Psalms 91 further expresses that:

For he will command his angels concerning you

to guard you in all your ways; they will lift you

up in their hands, so that you will not strike your

foot against a stone.

Then God empowers those who are in the secret place to do supernatural things. David continues his Psalms by writing some of his own testimony, by writing:

You will tread on the lion and the cobra; you

will trample the great lion and The serpent.

"Because he loves me," says the Lord, "I

will rescue him; I will protect him for he

acknowledges my name. He will call on me,

and I will answer him; I will be with him in

trouble, I will deliver him and honor him. With

long life I will satisfy him, and show him my

salvation."

Crisis can happen to anyone at any time but it is how one handles it that makes one a victor or a victim; and when one prays he or she becomes an overcomer. Some might agree that crisis is the cause of bad choices, and are inevitable to groups of people doing illegal or unsociable things like: dealing drugs, prostitution, or criminal activity. The fact of the matter is that everyone at one point or another will suffer crisis. Others might make arguments that not everyone shares the same morals, social status, values, religious beliefs or financial statuses, as others makings some less prone to crisis than others. However, whatever the cause of crisis there is a Biblical answer that can lead people from diverse situations to their creator so they can attain good success. In this paper the crises that are presented in Kristi Kanels' book, "A Guide to Crisis Intervention" concern death, homelessness, homosexuality, etc.... will be explicated in this paper, along with the ideas of authors Clyde Narramore, Richard Olson, Wayne Oates and William Backus.

It is important that those dealing with crisis understand that there is hope when one seeks the help of a Pastor and also when one prays. A Pastor's role is to lead the sheep into a greener pasture, and when one seeks the advice or instruction of a God fearing leader it only leads to a better and successful future. In Jeremiah 12:11 the author writes how God desires that His people have a good end. Crisis should not dictate the end for God's' people.

The life of a human being is measured by the stages in which one lives, and the potential that each one displays while here on earth. The only creator of the human soul and body is God who fashioned man after His own image. Human beings choose to follow God their creator or their own wills but as Job said, "we came from dust and we will go back to dust;" however, the human soul must one-day face God and give an account for every deed done on this earth. This synopsis contains various authors and their viewpoints on the human life and the process of aging from pre-birth, children, adolescents and college students, adults, and the elderly; and, will explore what various authors Thomas Armstrong, George Vaillant, James Dobson, Sella Henry and Richard Jessor have to say about the various stages of aging.

Chapter 1:

"Understanding a Need for Counsel"

A Crisis is "a time of intense difficulty, trouble, or danger."[7] In Kristi Kanels' "A Guide to Crisis Intervention," the author discusses that people when people are in need of assistance they should seek the help of: Pastor, Secular, Professional or Medical help. Help comes from various sources and the best part about "help" is that it is available if one chooses to seek for it. Those that seek "help" are often better off and more successful than those who hide the issue and become more depressed and seek alternatives that are destructive like drugs, prostitution, or eventually commit suicide.

Kanel also included that there are four types of crisis, as follows:

1. A precipitating event occurs

2. A person has a perception of the event as threatening or damaging

---

[7] http://www.oxforddictionaries.com/us/definition/american_english/crisis

3. This perception leads to emotional distress

4.The emotional distress leads to impairment in functioning due to failure of an individual's coping methods that previously have prevented a crisis from occurring.

The Chinese meaning of the word *crisis* means both danger and opportunity; because, people can come out either productive or unproductive based on the way one chooses to deal with the situation. I feel that if one prays while in crises the outcome would be for the better; regardless, how difficult the crisis. In order for one to develop there must be crisis. Crisis situations according to Kanel usually cease within 4-6 weeks. The author also states that people cannot tolerate more than two weeks of extreme tension. When they are able to receive help they are able to stabilize and become stronger. When people receive no help they have a lower functioning than before for coping skills for future stressors. When a new stressor hits if they still do not receive help the individual becomes worst because they are at a newer state of disequilibrium and according to the author it lowers their level of functioning bringing on death or psychosis or a severe personality disorder. I feel that if a person receives the help needed they are able to regain hope and are more confident for future events. The Bible says in Proverbs 13:12 that, "Hope deferred maketh the heart sick: but when the desire cometh, it is a tree of life." When help is received it is like offering a person their life and livelihood back, thus making them stronger to deal with future stressors.

Lack of support can scar one's memory for the worst. It leaves the individual with feelings of abandonment, fear and lack of trust in people when one does not receive the needed help. The author Kanel might agree that an individual goes through the "learning process" when one discovers that one should seek help and intervention in a crisis situation. The author might agree that one has succeeded through crisis situations when one seeks for help and one may fail in times of crisis if one does not receive the help he needs in crisis.

In Narramore's writing he stresses the need for counseling and not just preaching. He believes that people need the one on one conversation with the Pastor, minister or teacher to help lead or direct their lives in a more productive manner. People struggling with homosexuality or straying away from the Lord might only receive a hint of the message preached on Sunday; in addition, they need follow up and someone to tell them how to get to the end of the tunnel that they are facing.

Chapter 2

"Ideas of Kristi Kanel:

Learning, Memory and Cognition"

Asking for Help

In *A Guide to Crisis Intervention* by Kristi Kane a crisis is, "an obstacle that is for a time insurmountable by the use of customary methods of problem solving." In Kristi Kanels' *A Guide to Crisis Intervention* the author discusses that when people are in need of assistance they should seek the help of a: Pastor, Secular professional or medical help. Help comes from various sources and the best part about help is that it is available from different sources. Those that seek help are often better off and more successful than those who hide the issue and become more depressed. Those who do not seek help might turn to destructive behaviors like drugs, or eventually commit suicide.

In dealing with crisis situations one might need the support of medication, family intervention or individual counseling. It is also recommended that one seeks help with an open and trusting mind while in counseling, because a counselor will seem like a threat if one is not received with an open mind. Also, the author feels that people should be surrounded by support group such as one's church, family, friends or work. The author terms the way a person perceives a situation as the cognitive key. In this situation the counselor is the one that gives needed information to the client about his or her situation in order to bring understanding about the person's crisis.

The author explains that there are two types of crisis: developmental and situational. Developmental crisis occurs throughout one's normal developmental process in maturing from one level in one's life to another. Situational crisis are the ones people find themselves in due to a change that they had no control over. The author Kanel recommends that those in distress or crisis situations seek help regardless if they have monetary support, or not. The author also recommends that people in need of help seek paraprofessionals and it is even recommended that the professional has at least a master's degree to give counsel to the medically ill.

Gerald Caplan's "Seven Characteristics of Effective Coping Behavior"

Crisis has varying degrees for different people for example those who do not seek help experience "a period of disorganized ensues, a period of upset, during which many abortive attempts at a solution are made."[8] In Kristi Kanels book, he included several keys that Gerald Caplan shared as his, "Seven Characteristics of Effective Coping Behavior" which are as follows:

1. Actively exploring reality issues and searching for information

2. Freely expressing both positive and negative feelings and tolerating frustration

---

[8] Kristi Kanel, A Guide to Crisis Intervention: What is a Crisis and Crisis Intervention (Stan Cengage Learning, 2015), 18.

3. Actively invoking help from others

4. Breaking problems into manageable bits and working through them one at a time

5. Being aware of fatigue and pacing coping efforts while maintaining control in as many areas

of functioning as possible

6. Mastering feelings where possible; being flexible and willing to change

7. Trusting in oneself and others and having a basic optimism about the outcome

One's memory is either scared for the worst when one does not receive the needed help due to the lack of resources or people's availability to help, or, memory is enhanced and confidence is gained so that an individual can cope with life's stressors and crisis with ease knowing that the key out of their dilemma is through asking for help. Behavior is the effect from one's outcome during crisis situations; because, it is the outcome that causes individuals to begin to *learn* how success is found or failure during a difficult situation. The author Kanel might agree that an individual goes through the "learning phases" when one discovers that seeking help and intervention in a crisis leads to victory.

Kanel might agree that when one develops a pattern of how to correctly deal crisis one would succeed and become an overcomer, vs. the one who constantly lives in misery, and failure because he feels asking for help seems pointless. Successful thinking occurs when one *learns* that asking for help during crisis situations leads one to victory. I believe Kanel, would agree that the absence of progress in crisis situations, unless there is a **miracle**, would lead one would failure. The only answer to stopping failure is to admit the need for help. Help is not belittling or degrading oneself for support; however, it is the complete opposite because it builds up and encourages one to succeed.

In, "A Guide to Crisis Intervention" that in order to succeed one must begin to develop higher functioning levels and confidence to deal with life's stressors; on the other hand, when a person walks in denial, repression or dissociation the author might agree that their *learning* process is gradually becoming lower than before.

Ideas on Cognition with Kanel

When an individual finds themselves going further into failure, their *cognition* needs to change. The *cognition* of an individual is disastrous if bent on failure. According to the Oxford Dictionary, failure is the absence of success. When one fails to do better it is because his *cognition* tells him that it is ok to digress to drugs, promiscuous behavior, etc. One's thinking or *cognition* changes when it is challenged through the Godly counsel of a Pastor or Spiritual leader. Those that fail to seek for counsel fail because they choose to keep poor *cognition*. *Cognition* is not ingrained through DNA, but a pattern of bad choices, habits or alternatives chosen when dealing with life's stressors. It is apparent in society today that many people choose to go to the bar when stressed at work, or, hire a prostitute when faced with family problems. To many alternatives are available to people in society today and very few are seeking God or Godly counsel when dealing with issues such as their marriage, children, bad relationships, etc....

The call for holiness needs to be made today to help those suffering so that they do not end up in a hopeless estate without God. People inevitably seek for help whether in the bar chair in front of the beer maker or at a counseling session; however, the differences are enormous. One situation might lead an individual into cardiac arrest because he drank himself away or for the other, a stable and structured marriage life. The choice that one makes is based on one's *cognition*. If one has poor cognition one's situation gets lower and one's thinking leads to depression and worst of all, suicide. Denying help or not seeking help in crisis situations will only worsen one's situation. The author might agree that one has succeeded through crisis situations when one seeks the professional help of a Pastor, and one only fails when he fails to ask for help in crisis situations.

Cognition is the mental action or process of acquiring knowledge and understanding through thought, experience, and the senses.[9] There are different ways that people learn to understand why things happen and how to succeed even in times of crisis. Some of the models or theories in Kristi Kane's "A Guide to Crisis

---

[9]Oxford Dictionaries, s.v. "cognition," accessed November 1, 2015, http://www.oxforddictionaries.com/us/

Intervention" are the Psychoanalytic Theory, the Existential

Theory, the Humanistic Approach, the Cognitive- Behavioral

Theories, Brief Therapy, Critical Incident debriefing and the ABC

Model of Crisis Intervention.

In the Psychoanalytic Theory the counselor might

encourage the victim in crisis that their psychic ability was

consumed and they have no more physic ability to deal with

disaster. People with personality disorders are told that their

psychic abilities were used up by dealing with their disorder and

have no more ability to deal with disasters at hand. People with

personality disorders or psychic disorders usually cannot deal with

their problems at hand because they use all of their energy to deal

with previous stressors.

In the Existential Theory the counselor might suggest that

throughout anyone's life experience that stressors and crises occur, but they can gain opportunities through a crisis situation. In this theory it is believed that good can come out of a terrible situation.

Kanel would believe that it is important for the individual to realize the need for help. For example, a person cannot receive counsel unless they sign up for counseling sessions, because they have to first admit that there may be a problem to deal with, and then go to a counselor to help them navigate to get the answer. For them to receive their breakthrough or their answer to prayer they have to first be willing to seek help or advice by admitting there is a problem. Kanel might agree that crisis arise as an opportunity to seek for direction and help; similar, to Olson who believes that those who sought the help of Jesus ended up healed, delivered or made whole.

In this book the author is describing how adverse situations can cause people to react differently in their lives in order to cope with crisis. In the Church author Wayne E. Oates explains how even Christians wear mask to hide their true feelings, or identity from others in the Church. They might do excessive activities in the Church or back down completely while only attending. However, the root issues should be dealt with in counseling in order to restore the person completely to be successful in their situation.

Backus explains that in the church history that people are used to casting out devils; however, he sees the need to also give medication in the church. He feels that if more people had the opportunity to get their proper treatment that they might be able to gain more help that they need. The author gives advice on who is qualified to counsel.

Chapter 3

"Ideas of Clyde Narramore:

Concerning Learning, Memory and Cognition"

Narramore might say that *cognition* begins in counseling; and, *learning* takes place in the Sunday morning preaching services. One is able to get, or, be directed to advice by "one on one" counseling with a Pastor, a medical professional or seeking legal help from an attorney. With the guidance of knowledgeable and professional counselors one can receive the assistance needed.

The author brings out the point that Jesus took time to counsel those in need like Zacchaeus in Luke 19:2, the woman at the well in John 4:6, and many others in which He took out personal time to deal with their needs "one on one." In these cases, the people left completely delivered because their whole lifestyle changed after their encounter with Jesus. People became aware of their sin and changed immediately after their encounter with the Lord. Counsel offers better alternatives. When good counsel is followed it causes the individuals in crisis situations to succeed, ultimately, bringing God glory from the success in the

lives of people. The Bible says in Proverbs 24:6, "For by wise counsel thou shalt make thy war: and in multitude of counselors there is safety." Change happens when Pastors take the time to offer counseling for their congregations just as Jesus did with those who met Him.

The author suggests in, "Psychology of Christian Counseling" that counselors should be competent, professional, one of good reputation, dependable, and one that knows God. When a counselor has professional attire, and a respectable reputation it helps those in need to desire counseling. An individual can begin to *learn* how to become a better person and how to achieve in their everyday situations as they attend their counseling sessions. Congregants are able to *learn* what God's perfect plan for their lives are when they are open to receive counsel and direction from their Pastors.

What Activates Successful Thinking

When people choose to accept counsel they use it when necessary. It is up to the individual to keep what they learn in *memory* so that they can succeed. Successful Thinking should be activated in one's memory by rehearsing and applying positive counsel when stressors present themselves throughout one's life. A Pastor's job is to lead a flock and when people keep that in *memory it* would make it easier for the sheep to seek for help in times of crisis. Confusion decreases when congregants begin to see the Pastor as their mentor, teacher or guide. God gives Pastors insight and direction on how to lead so that the flock or congregation can see God's blessings in their lives; however, when congregants are not willing to receiving this mentorship they begin to seek for understanding elsewhere and become those with itchy ears and a hardened heart thus leading them into depression and worst scenarios than they started with. Successful thinking is a choice, and one must choose to keep in memory good alternatives when crisis presents itself.

Good counselors also activate successful thinking. "To be good counselors we must first be the right kind of people ourselves. We must let the Lord take charge of our lives."[10] Author Clyde Narramore, believes that a counselor's lifestyle should line up with the Word of God, and be led of the Holy Spirit to counsel effectively. Counselors have a high status in society because they are looked upon as the ones with all the answers; as well as, one's personal life which is reviewed as a book by all those in the congregation. In James 3:17, James writes, "But the wisdom that is from above is first pure, then peaceable, gentle, and

---

[10] Clyde Narramore, Psychology of Christian Counseling: The Counselor (Pasadena, A Division of Harper Collins Publishers, 1960), 19.

easy to be entreated, full of mercy and good fruits, without partiality, and without hypocrisy." The counseling ministry should be delivered from a Spirit filled believer; because, the advice from an unbeliever is of satan. The author Clyde Narramore, gives an illustration of a lady who had gone through a crisis situation and sought the counsel of an unbeliever. His advice to her was to live it up and enjoy her life by doing what feels good. This humanistic approach to dealing with life's problems Narramore calls Satanic.

Narrramore thinks that counsellors should be trustworthy because they are privileged to confidential information. The author states that the counselor should not argue with the counselee because it can cause the counselee to build up barriers. In this area of counseling the counselee might remember being argued with and avoid further counseling sessions, or refuse to discuss certain matters that are necessary for healing to take place. Another important factor is to eliminate partiality when counseling, because one could send the wrong advice. It is important for counselors to be Spirit filled, professional and in a good state with God to minister to people.

Important Pointers for Counselors

Narramore recommends that counselors are prepared to counsel by: setting an appointment, preparing an interview, beginning an interview, determining the length of the interview, closing the interview, recording the interview, and handling persistent cases. In the "The Psychology for Counseling" Clyde Narramore stresses that the counselor operates professionally. It is important that the counselee can look up to or respect the counselor and it is recommended that counseling takes place in an office or in a place of privacy. In order to keep the counselee encouraged in seeking counsel it is important that the sessions and the information gathered should be kept confidential and only shared with a deacon if prayer is needed. When information is exposed from a counseling session it gives the counselee a feeling of despair, because a breach of trust has been broken. It is essential that all notes be locked away so that other church members and staff are not able to access the notes from counseling sessions.

It is important that the counselor has set appropriate time limits so that those seeking help do not feel rushed. In this way they can return to recap or continue where they left off. By setting time limits counselors do not have to feel as if they offended the person being counseled by cutting off too soon; however, the time frame should be discussed so that everyone is aware of the time that the session will occur. The counselor is allowed to help the counselee find answers not expose their innermost issues with the congregation. It is advised in Narramore's book that Counselors should not preach or make examples from those seeking counsel with the Pastor. This hinders a person's progress because others would feel the Pastor is talking about the individual that is being counseled or the counselee would immediately become suspicious

that the Pastor is making them a public illustration.

Chapter 4

"Ideas of Richard Olson:

Concerning Learning, Memory and

Cognition"

In this book, "Ask Anything a Pastoral Theology of Inquiry" the author aware readers that Jesus also asked questions. This implies that it is ok to ask a question if you need an answer even if you might think you know the answer. The author describes how throughout the Gospels Jesus was asked questions and replied about 200 times with a question. Author Olson also makes it known that the Bible was not descriptive in punctuation throughout the gospels which gives him the idea that other questions might have been made. In counseling sessions, the counselee has to feel ok with asking questions and the counselor should feel free to also ask questions back. Both the counselor and the counselee should be free to ask questions. The author implies in his text that readers should not be afraid to ask questions of text or respond to questions with questions. In using this approach, the counselee can learn from their counseling session.

The author added that Jesus used the method of questioning

to communicate deep truths to people. The author understands the Omnipotence and the All Knowingness of Jesus; however, he shows that in asking questions he related powerful truths to probe the minds of seeking individuals. Jesus wanted His followers and disciples to *learn* and make logical conclusions based on their own findings and mindsets. Jesus asked the disciples in Mark 8, "Whom do men say that I the Son of man am?" then turned around and asked, "But whom say ye that I am?" to get them to actively try to figure out His identity on their own. It is not as if Jesus did not know His identity, but he wanted His disciples to begin to reason on their own in order to *learn* of Jesus. They learned of Jesus and began to draw their own conclusions based on their findings in friendship, seeing His divine nature of performing miracles, and understanding His divinity.

It is Safe to Ask

Dr. Olson believes that Jesus answers the questions of His

followers through His parables; ultimately, these parables them to their answers. Dr. Olson studies and expounds on several parables from the book of John, and he expresses what Jesus means by answering with questions or parables. The parables that Jesus gives provokes His listeners to try and figure out hidden meanings. The author expresses that some might believe questioning the Bible is doubting the Bible; however, he navigates through John exposing how questioning could unlock secrets and hidden information that Jesus gives to His disciples through questioning. The Book of John portrays Jesus as the Son of God, the Divine Teacher, Soul Winner, Bread of Life, Water of Life and more; however, He is willing to teach mere mortals how to become closer to God through provoking their intellect to discover the mysteries of God.

A Biblical example is in John 5:6, "When Jesus saw him lie, and knew that he had been now a long time in that case, He saith unto him, "Wilt thou be made whole?" Jesus was expressing a question to help that man out of his dilemma. There is a Biblical principle concerning receiving, and it is this: one must first ask in order to receive. In John 5, in order for the man to receive healing from Jesus he had to ask for it; for this reason, Jesus helps him receive his healing through asking him if he wants to "be made whole." Jesus said in John 16:24, "Hitherto have ye asked nothing in my name: ask, and ye shall receive, that your joy may be full." Jesus knows how to receive a gift at the Father's' hand and wants to help people in need of deliverance or healing by leading them into proper communication to the Father. In James 4:2, the scripture says, "...yet ye have not, because ye ask not." Jesus is continually teaching in the gospels the act of asking God for what one needs. In Matthew 7:7 it states, "Ask, and it shall be given you; seek, and ye shall find; knock, and it shall be opened unto you..." One's own breakthrough can be a question away; because, it is the act of asking, knocking, or seeking that exposes a need to the Deliverer. At times Jesus gave people the opportunity to get their own deliverance based on their desire to ask for it. The Canaanite woman in Matthew 15:26, asked for Jesus help pleased Jesus so much with her asking that He healed her possessed daughter. She understood that she had to overlook the shame associated with looking for help, because compared to Israel she was a dog; however, she reasons with Jesus knowing that dogs eat crumbs that children leave behind, and ask for them to gain her daughter's healing. How desperate does one need to be to forget the shame that is connected with asking and just simply "ask for help!"

A person cannot receive counsel unless they sign up for counseling sessions, because they have to first admit that there is a problem and then ask for help. For anyone to receive their breakthrough or their answer to prayer they must be willing to ask for help. Kanel might agree that crisis arise as an opportunity to seek for direction and help; similar, to Olson he believes that those who seeking Jesus' help were healed, delivered or made whole.

Chapter 5

"Ideas of Wayne Oates:

Concerning Learning, Memory and

Cognition"

In "Behind the Mask Personality Disorders in Religious Behavior" Wayne E. Oates, is describing how adverse situations can cause people to react differently in their lives in order to cope with crisis. In the Church author Wayne E. Oates explains how even Christians wear mask to hide their true feelings, or identity from others in the Church. They might do excessive activities in the Church or back down completely while only attending. However, the root issues should be dealt with in counseling in order to restore the person completely to be successful in their situation. The author describes how diverse situations would cause people to react in ways that could be easily spotted in ministry. Wearing a mask is the façade that one might use to pretend that all is well; yet, in all actuality one might be in need of, "help."

The Root of Dependency

The author begins by expressing that everyone in the start of their lives are dependent upon their parents. He shows that dependency is a natural part of the human's existence. Until one is brave and matures to the level where they can live independently, he or she is dependent upon one's' parent. He also makes it evident that children should strive not to bring shame or dishonor to their parents by bad choices that they could make in adulthood, because it could reflect shame on the parents as if they lacked parenting skills. Dependency helps children become more stable and allow children to lead better lives because they imitate what they are taught in childhood.

The author describes that those who are dependent as adults are very agreeable, likable and would do anything the way you want it done just to please you; however, he compares this characteristic to those who become like clones of the ones they are following. These people are often caught in a trap according to Oates because everything they desire or need is looked for in this person. The author describes that this dependent nature of an individual could be dangerous, because as with Hitler he caused a whole group of people to imitate him to the point of destroying others.

A dependent person the author might agree sees themselves as the person they might idolize. This type of behavior causes the person to see no great accomplishments of their own; but, only in others and this is dehumanizing, because it causes an individual to cease being human. In creation it was not God's will to create robots. The *cognition* of the dependent person is to portray the desires, motivations and accomplishments of the ones that they might idolize in order to reach what they might feel success; and, to the dependent person that is to emulate the person they idolize. When one seeks to please God instead of people they can avoid the problems of changing their personality to suit people. People can change their attitudes and opinions about others due to success, money or fame; sad to say, their opinions might change about you when you lose your job, car and house. God's opinions of us never changes; therefore, the ultimate goal of any believer should be to please God.

The author feels that people suffering from personality disorders in the church mentally understand and make themselves believe that their ideas, or desires are not good enough to follow; in turn, *learn* to become like others who they deem important. They learn to emulate and follow the desires and dictates of those they depend on because they feel that their choices are inferior. Dependent people often *remember* how to be a clone by emulating what they see their idol doing and thus become that person's clone. In doing this their lives are not individualistic, but a copy of the one they intend to follow. In their memory they feel that they are successful once they become like the one they are following.

Author Oates in his writings describes that the dependent sees themselves as weak or fragile and feel that those superior are allowed to treat them however they choose. This idea of low self-esteem or low self-worth the author states should be contrary Genesis 1:27 which says, "Christians are made in the image and likeliness of God."

Chapter 6

"Ideas of Dr. William Backus:

Concerning Learning, Memory and

Cognition"

According to, "Telling the Truth to Troubled People" by William Backus, it explains that in church history that people cast out devils; however, he sees the need to also give medication in the church. He feels that if more people had the opportunity to get their proper treatment that they might be able to gain more help that they need. The author gives advice on who is qualified to counsel. Counseling is important and he believes it belongs in the church; however, he believes that the person must be qualified to counsel. In order to counsel the author, Backus believes that one must be lead of the Holy Spirit. He does not believe that every minister in church should counsel. Also, he feels that they should operate in the gift of knowledge sometimes. The author also believes that most of the ministry of a counselor should be done outside of the counseling walls and in intercessory prayer. He thinks that counselors should desire to pray for their counselees and that if they do not desire to pray they should not counsel. The author thinks that those called to counsel should also be trained because they must have the proper training to do so in a school.

What Qualifies to Counsel

Backus believes, if a person feels that they are called to counsel they should first have the knowledge of fundamental Christian teaching, have training in prescriptive psychopathology, know about various clinical treatments, know all about the beliefs in self-talk in generating human behavior, and know from the place of experience the place of belief in the Christian life it's transforming power when its objects is truth, and the methods for helping others is to share this power. The author believes that counselors should be well rounded in all areas and scopes in the counseling so that they are able to lead those in need of help, whether it be psychological, spiritual, and emotional or just some encouragement to make the next step forward. Counseling is for everyone who desires to ask for help.

The author suggests that those desiring to counsel start humbly by allowing themselves to be monitored for training as they begin. This way they could receive guidelines and pointers on how they might counsel to help those individuals seeking their help. He points out that all professionals starting out begin under mentorship and monitoring and he feels that counselors should take that approach as well to be successful in aiding those who desire help.

Chapter 7:

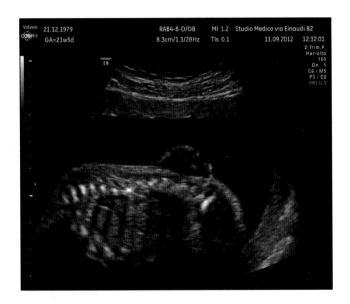

"Pre-Birth"

The existence of man, contrary to human believe begins in the womb. A whole life and world seemingly undiscovered exist in the hidden memory of every individual. In the Holy Scriptures God said, "Before I formed you in the womb I knew you, and before you were born I consecrated you; I appointed you a prophet to the nations." The Psalmist David said, "Upon you I have learned from before my birth; you are he who took me from my mother's womb. My praise is continually of you." Meaning that David knew of God's help towards Him yet while in the womb and he remembers his experience of being in the womb. In Dr. Thomas Armstrong's, "The Human Odyssey" he discusses issues of the human existence using poetry, epics, religion, and science. It challenges different ideologies of the human existence and causes one to think of the various definitions of human existence held throughout history.

In Chapter 1, the author begins by sharing a Jewish story of how a person's destiny is revealed through a bright light while in the womb. The baby then loses all memory when the Angel Laila strikes her finger on the baby's upper lip causing an indentation on it. It is concluded that when a person forgets or misplaces something then remembers they touch this indentation on the lip and exclaim, "Ah yes, now I remember!" This belief supports the idea that our unconscious lives in the womb might not have been unconscious at all, but forgotten. The poet Samuel Taylor, did write about how the 9-month period that precedes a person's life is much more adventurous than the 3 score and 10 years after.

The fate of a human as a sperm traveling through the fallopian tube is animated as a quest for one's life. The author uses life illustrations to explore what could have been happening in the womb. The takeoff of the sperm is compared to a mega-marathon to the moon using the entire population of 3 large states. The analogy shows how vast the population is that is competing for fertilization, and only one sperm gets the prize. The battle for life seems so competitive in the womb being that all others die or are misplaced in scar tissue in the fallopian tube. Therefore, each life is precious being that it was the strongest to survive this fight for life in the womb. In African myths the first humans were lowered from the sky to earth. This could parallel the existence of Adam and Eve only that they were created by the dust of the earth; unlike the rest of us, they did not have to fight for their existence in the womb.

In becoming a fetus, the baby resembles all aspects of creatures from sea life, amphibians and mammals. The author suggest the human spine curls up like a shrimp. The body is said to take on new forms at different periods to help equip the body to build on neurons and functions so that the fetus begins to look like an adult. Some believe that the human soul is present in a fetus once a mother feels sensations in her womb and the fetus begins to move. Other cultures believe the tree of life is wrapped around the mother's umbilical cord. The author Dr. Armstrong describes the carrying of a womb as a hellish or heavenly like experience. Wombs in where the mother desires her baby are nurtured, receive good foods, hear songs and receives the enjoyment of both parents. However, in wombs where the fetus is unwanted experiences rejection hormones like anger, recreational drugs, alcohol, and sexually transmitted diseases. Dr. Armstrong also noted how Leonardo da Vinci and Salvador Dali reported remembering the hellish experience in the womb. This is thought to have been caused by the mother's desire to abort the child but might have been restricted by laws to abort the fetus. It is also noted that high levels of oxytocin are released by the mother and child just before birth, and that it has an amnesic effect. The author compares this to the angel Lailah touching the upper lip causing the fetus to forget its past life in the womb, while preparing to exit the womb.

My thoughts go to children who are aborted, they fully experience the knowledge of the death and rejection of their mothers.

Are traumatic birthing experiences affect a person's life? Dr. Armstrong might agree with the idea that trauma at birth could affect a person's life. He records Thomas Hobbes birthing experience and his analogy with a life filled with fear and trauma. Hobbes claims that his mother gave birth to twins, himself and fear. He felt his entire career through life reflected fear due to the fact that his mother went into labor when she heard the Spanish Armada was about to invade England. Fearful or traumatic experiences may influence the personality traits of a child's future based on this personal experience documented by Hobbes.

Furthermore, Dr. Armstrong documents that the birthing

experience is numbered and filled with chemicals once in the hospital; thus, stopping the communication between mother and fetus to send out her baby into the world. A mother's bond is to naturally allow the child to communicate and send signals to the moon on the best timing to send their child out into the world. The idea of birth changes as technology and the human mind progress. No longer do people have home births only, or sit on a stool while the baby rolls out into a hole in the earth. Today moms choose to have science help them deliver their babies with the assistance of medication, give birth in a swimming pool, or choose to take no medication while holding the husband's hand and scream. The birthing process is so diverse but it is recorded that in the Netherlands midwives assist at home pregnancies and have lower death rate of 4.96 in each 1,000 births; while in the US hospitals

6.43 deaths occur to each 1,000 babies born in the US.

Dr. Stanislav Grof, explains the birthing process as the four

primary stages of, "Basic Perinatal Matrices (BPMs)." In these

stages he expresses the experiences a human being under the use of

LSD while it was still legal in the US. In Stage 1 of the, "Basic

Perinatal Matrix One" subjects reported whether they were in a

good womb vs. a bad womb; in other words, a good womb with

feelings of happiness and wellbeing, vs. a bad womb with feelings

of rejection and fear. In the next stage of BPMII subjects felt

trapped and confined because the uterus is contracting but the

cervix is not fully dilated. In the third stage the subjects reported a

death like experience as they are traveling through a tunnel filled with blood. In the final stage the umbilical cord is cut and subjects

feel a sense of rebirth and expansion. These stages were recorded

showing that babies feel trauma and pain during the birthing

experience just as the mom. A woman also forgets the pain of her

birth after the experience in John 16:21 it says, "A woman giving

birth to a child has pain because her time has come; but when her

baby is born she forgets the anguish because of her joy that a child

is born into the world."

Chapter 8:

"Children"

In Dr. James Dobson's, "The New Strong-Willed Child he reports receiving some of the most hostile notes from children, because they did not like being spanked; however, spankings are God's' divine will for children to be trained and taught to behave. One kid replied, "Roses are Red, violets are blue, I got spanked because of you." Dr. Dobson developed 6 steps in rearing a "strong-willed" child. The first stage is teaching the child to respect authority. If a child feels himself a "conqueror" when there is a match between himself and his parents he will lose respect for his parents. Dr. Dobson recorded the testimony of a mother who bore 19 children. She explains conquering their will and gaining the respect of a child is important in child rearing. By letting down one's guard and giving into a child one allows them to see how far one is willing to let them go.

Setting boundaries is a topic that Dr. Dobson stresses in his teaching because it helps the child to understand the concept of the word "no." When a parents chooses to be passive it is the worst thing that a parent can do according to Ms. Wesley; because, it only leads to much harsher discipline as they grow older. Ms. Wesley believes that the child's will should be conquered early, because once the child matures it turns into stubborn and defiant behavior towards their parents. It benefits the child if his or her behavior is addressed earlier on in their life.

Chapter 9:

"Adolescence and College Students"

The age of the adolescence seems to have so many twist and turns and might be perceived as one of the toughest parts of development for an individual. At this age one is aware of choices and is allowed to make several decisions; and this is where one chooses to replicate behaviors seen at home, follow crowds, exemplify positive or negative behaviors, etc.... The author Richard Jessor, of "Problem –Behavior Theory" believes that the behavior problems among adolescents, or young teens and college students is the use of alcohol and tobacco. The author suggest certain factors increase problem behavior in teens and colleges students such as, "low parental disapproval of problem behavior, higher peep approval of problem behavior, high peer models for problem behavior, low parental controls and support, low peer controls, low compatibility between parent and peer expectations, and low parent (relative to peer) influence."

The author suggest that adolescence should develop or be taught "values, expectations, beliefs, attitudes, and orientations towards self and society." Also, the author encourages the idea that all adolescents should be involved in church and school going them a positive place to interact and grow good behaviors.

Author Jessor also structured a problem-behavior theory framework consisting of: the perceived- environment system, the personality system and the behavior system. This is where the author connects low parental oversight and boundaries with high exposure to problem behavior type practices, such as alcohol abuse, cigarettes, tobacco, sexual intercourse, etc.... The personality system is developed by one's beliefs, values,

expectations, etc.… The author's concept of problem behaviors

and conventional behaviors stem with the actual involvement of

promiscuous behaviors. Conventional behaviors are accepted in

society as the norm for adolescence, like attending church or going

to school. While problem behavior stem from the adolescence *will*

to go against the grain and drink alcohol, smoke cigarettes, engage

in sexual intercourse and use marijuana.

The author argues what might be identified as a problem

behavior for an adolescence seen as a norm alcohol is a problem

behavior while it is legal for those over the age of 18. Intercourse

is practiced by adults but adolescents should be refrained from

participating in sexual acts. The author found that the more antisocial negative behaviors are present that the less prosocial behaviors, such as going to church and getting health occur. To enhance negative behaviors, the author, suggest that adolescence get routine medical care, have more positive parental influence, attend church service, have an increased value for educational improvement, etc. The author also suggests that if positive role models are around adolescence and positive influences it may alter bad or negative behaviors in youth.

Chapter 10:

"Adults"

One of the most amazing statements that stood out in George Vaillant's, *Aging Well* was the statement, "No successful aging is not an oxymoron." It is apparent his entire theses are wrapped up in this statement. There is a good way to age as well as a bad way and those that age successfully benefit from a long, fruitful and positive life. Although, they might be sick he stresses the importance that their goal is getting better and going on with their life. On the other hand, those that age poorly is sick, have miserable lives and have horrible health conditions due to alcohol or tobacco use. He records ideas and thoughts of people that he studies throughout his book. One person stated that aging for him was, "to live, to work, to learn something that I didn't know yesterday-to enjoy the precious moments with my wife."

The author saw that with another person he studied that

although she had a horrible past she forgave and grew healthy and aged well. The author surmised that forgiveness leads to successful aging. Anthony Pirelli was one of the author's studies who grew up poor, in a single household, family that had limited income and did not speak English. Yet, this man went to school, learned English and became an accountant and lived a healthy lifestyle; however, he suffered a coronary bypass surgery and stroke. When asked about his past he expressed the gift of forgiveness and forgave his mother who suffered from manic depression disorder and understood that she could not supervise their progress in school because she did not speak English. Also, he complimented his father as a good family man that would do anything for his family.

The author has a unique way of thinking about sickness, he says "Objective good physical health was less important to successful aging than the subjective good health. By this I mean that it is all right to be ill as long as you do not feel sick." The author also includes ideas from Robert Browning who believes that aging causes one to become better by growing from past experience s, by assuming life only gets better as it is lived. It leads people to believe that the best potential of a person is found in their old age, by growing older. In Shakespeare's, "As you Like It" Shakes spheres depiction of old age is confusion and loss of memory of one's life. It makes life seem meaningless and as a gamble. The author makes King Lear who is aging seem foolish, senile and without any recollection of his life. Dr. Vaillant believes successful aging should emit joy vs. unsuccessful aging in King Lear's dilemma. An 84-year-old study member replied to Dr. Vaillant that she believed, "Positive aging means to love, to work, to learn something we did not know yesterday, and to enjoy the remaining precious moments with loved ones."

In the study of Adult development there were 3 groups that were studied in the process of aging well. The first group consisted of 268 socially advantaged Harvard graduates born about 1920 (This group had the longest prospective of mental and physical health). The next group were 456 socially disadvantaged inner city men born about 1930 (this group had the largest prospective study of "blue collar" adult development in the world.) The Final group was 90 middle class intellectually gifted women born about 1910 (the longest prospective development of women in the world). A grant was given to Harvard University that allowed two individuals Arlie Bock and Clark Health, student health service physicians to study Health Development, by philanthropist William T. Grant. They screened Harvard Sophomores in 1920 and eliminated students with mental health issues or demonstrated poor academic success. Thy chose 248 men to screen throughout their lives they screened members of their households as well. Most prospects were white men whose parents were born in the U.S. out of this population 4 men ran for senate.

In the second study, Sheldon Glueck, a law professor received funding to conduct a case study on 500 boys that went to reform school and had not been in any legal trouble. In this study, Sheldon Glueck and wife Eleanor, as a social worker followed these men at ages 17, 25, and 32. They found similarities in economic issues such as growing up in families that did not own showers or tubs, the use of welfare and being known to 5 or more welfare agencies. Many of the boys repeated grades 2 or more ties and had parents from other states than the US. By the age of 60 only 2 of the 456 men remained alive. This study helped produce 2 books, "Unraveling Juvenile Delinquency," and "Crime in the Making" written by criminologist John Laub and Robert Sampson.

In the final sample the Terman Women were studied by Lewis Terman a professor of Education at Sanford University. He tried to find all students with an IQ of 140 or higher. His case study revealed that they were mostly gifted women; however, all private schools or biracial schools were excluded from his study for prejudice reasons of the society of that day. The woman subjected to the test lived relatively happy lives and married and the siblings did not suffer from half the childhood mortalities as other children their age. By the end of the study 111 of the 672 women were still alive after around 70 years.

The Termen women lived to be about 70-79, while the Harvard students were over 80 years of age. In the study of the Inner City men they lived from 60-69. The mortality of the Inner-city men from ages 68-79 was the same as the Terman and Harvard cohorts at age 78-80. The 29 Inner-City men who graduated from college was identical at age 70 to the Health of Harvard College graduates at age 70. The study showed that the less education, more obesity, greater alcohol and cigarette use were greater among Inner-city students which caused rapid decline of Health.

This retrospective study helped the investigators to analyze human health among their three groups. College education is one of the greatest factors among those who lived past 70. Those who lived to 60 abused alcohol or cigarettes or were obese. The educational levels of all groups proved that if one lived in the slumps or was born privileged as a Harvard graduate that one can live a healthy lifestyle. However, the quality of life is affected by one's consummation of alcohol and cigarettes or too much consummation of food.

At the death of Arlie Bock the files were transferred to the author of this book, "Aging Well" who saw the files as reunions with the people over a series of time with the Harvard Men, Inner City Students, and the Termen Women. He found those happy with life were easy to work with; while, those who were unloved hard to work with because they made him feel inferior or insecure and he found himself doing all the work as they gave so little he claimed and they received so much.

The author states that the study of adult development cost millions of dollars to keep open for 6-8 decades. The author also states it took good luck for Joe DiMaggio to hit safely in56 consecutive games. Also, many studies have fallen victim to the original victims dying. However, perseverance kept the study going to maturation. Also, the expense of the members who without them could not keep this study alive.

Eric Erickson, is recorded as the first social scientist to see aging as progression not decline. Shakespeare viewed aging in one of his plays as, "As so, from hour we ripe, / and then from hour to hour we rot and rot." Erick Ericson also believed after age 50 that one's life is not a downward staircase, but a widening one. I believe Erickson's belief that aging over 50 is a widening staircase, because one now has a network of relatives underneath oneself which causes one to be outgoing, a people's person and satisfied in life, because one shares one's experiences to those underneath oneself.

Author Vaillant also included Robert Havinghursts' Theory

on aging as developmental task, which are identity, intimacy, career consolidation, generativity, keeper of meaning and integrity. The first stage is identity which helps one to lose the holds of reliance or dependence on institutions and one's parents; and, to find a family to develop one's owns values and identity of where one might belong. Intimacy is the next stage, which is the ability to cohabit with another partner and exchange resources to help each other and having sexual a relationship with an individual over a decade. The third stage is career consolidation and this is an act of selfishness because one seeks to develop one's self; however, the author argue that one would be "selfless" if one does not develop this stage. The fourth stage is generativity which is assuming the role of a mentor, coach, or consultant to a younger person. Which is similar to the role of a parent that loosely guides his child. The fifth stage is keeper of meaning which is where one would keep traditions and values that one might find important such as religious beliefs and culture. Also, in this stage one would encourage the younger generations not to forsake God. The final stage consists of integrity where it is compared to wisdom and acceptance of one's life and its cycle. One understands that while the body decays wisdom remains.

Susan Wellcome was one of the Women in the study who grew up in the middle class and went to college. Her life was influenced by the constant rejection of her mother. If her mother accepted and loved her she might have completed college, learned the piano and lived more financially secure. However, she dropped out of college, dropped out of nursing school and refused learning to play the piano. However, her marriage healed her wounds and she began to soar in her personal life, marriage, and eventually went back to school. I feel her life could be in a movie like a romantic love story titled, "Love: The Power to Heal."

Bill Loman started a very well of to be lifestyle. He attended Harvard University with his brother and both were chosen or the case study. However, Bill Loman was an alcoholic and his health was constantly in decline. He died while working 40 hours a week and never married, because he stayed close to home. He did not get to advance to the level of Intimacy because he did not want to leave home. He had no grandchildren, barely gave, went to church on Christmas only with his mother and generated no

friends due to his alcohol ridden lifestyle.

Chapter 11:

"Elders"

In the introduction of, "The Eldercare Handbook" by Stella Henry she expresses her concerns for her parents and how they died. He fathers died at home as her mother requested; however, the author placed the mom in a nursing home until she died. Choices like these I believe should be asked and addressed while the parent is functioning so that the person left to care for them know exactly what to do for them if they are in that position. However, if the children are preoccupied with family and jobs it could be an overwhelming task; but, I think love for one's parents should ultimately lead an individual to make the right choice in caring for their parents.

The author owns a retirement home and she included the feelings and stories of families battling with the choice to put their parents into a retirement home. One of her first examples were

Victor and Grace were married 62 years and the mother needed

dialysis 3 times a day, a daily bath and change of clothes; however,

he was in the nursing home office with his son because he could

not care for her anymore. This is a decision of choice I believe the

son could have made better arrangements for her in his home. It

might be time consuming to set up a patient on a machine for

dialysis, but if people would take a moment to think that this

person changed my diapers once for 5 or more times a day it might

not seem so time consuming after all. I think the father was doing

a great job, but he was crying out for his son's help, and not to

finalize his wife's position in a nursing home.

Another family struggling with that decision was Jeanne

and her mom. Jeanne an executive was so involved in her life that

a friend had to remind of the condition of her 79-year-old mother

suffering from dementia. I feel society is moving so rapidly that

those who are unable to keep up get swept under a rug or put away

in a retirement home to free their loved ones of burdens.

Eventually Jeanne put her mom in a retirement home.

One of the common conceptions the elderly has when sent

into the nursing home is one of abandonment and that is what

Valerie did to her mom. Valerie was very explosive concerning her

mother's treatment and medical care. The worst part about it is

that the nursing home had to become her mother's ally just so that

she could receive proper treatment. The daughter insisted that the mother did not need to be put on a breathing machine to prolong her condition because she needed to go and not be held up to prolong her existence. Eventually, Valerie gave in and allowed the nursing home to care for her mother, but it took them a fight.

Another family was Debby and her husband. They chose to put the mother in a retirement home because she wet the couch and walked in on them one night in their bedroom. This judgment was harsh because the mother was knowledgeable on what was going on and had a terrible time adjusting to the environment. Vindictive behaviors make the elderly feel as if they are being punished. The mother had wet the couch once and the entire family drew the line and sent her off to the nursing home.

In some cases, I think the nursing home might be

appropriate. Laura cared for and loved her husband; however, he was becoming senile and abusive. Her choice was to admit him to the nursing home was a good one to protect herself from his hostile behavior; because, when she tried to push him away he got injured and sent to the hospital. With the help the retirement home she was able to see her husband in a controlled environment and she was able to help care for him.

In another case an 80-year-old son was caring for his 98-year-old mother. In this case they were both very old and the mother would not eat. She was extremely old and feeble yet her son saw that if she would not eat she would starve. In this case he sent his mother to the nursing home so that they could try to give her nutrition.

In this handbook chapter 2 records warning signs that adult children should look for in caring for their parents to detect early warning signs and seek help for their parent. The ten red flags to watch for with the elderly is: personal care, housekeeping, meals and appetite, memory, communication, mobility, depression, medication, finances and driving. Insufficiencies in any area or concerns are recommended to seek help if one is unable to care for your parents.

"Conclusion"

In Conclusion, some might conclude money, status or power makes one crisis situation different from the other; but, all people according to Kristi Kanel struggle and crisis happens to all at one point or another in their life. Crisis arise as a point of desperation or need in an individual's life in which he or she was not prepared. A slogan that I have always remembered was "Preparation precedes blessings." When one is prepared crisis seem to occur a lot less in that individual's life. In Matthew 25 it talks about the coming of the Lord is a blessing for those who are prepared; yet, a crisis for those who are not. The ten virgins were given a mandate to be ready with oil in their lamps but several did not take oil. Unfortunately, those virgins who did not take oil in their lamps missed out on their eternal Salvation, because they did not think it necessary to have oil in their lamps with their vessels. The Bible admonishes all Christians to be prepared for the coming of the Lord, because He might come as a thief in the night;

however, many Christians do not attend Church or participate in Church activities.

The Bible admonishes believers to pray without ceasing and I feel whatever the situation one might be facing prayer gives one power and victory to see success and a good end. I also feel similar to William Backus that Good counselors would be Spirit lead and people of prayer to seek God's perfect will concerning counseling an individual. I think prayerlessness in all situation lead to failure.

Ultimately, all life at every stage is important and not to be undermined. Each level is capable for greatness and the fulfilling of great things. God created humans to exemplify His glory and without God man is futile to live a life of bad choices and ultimately die without joy and God's' assurance of hope. Life was only explored to the final point of man on earth in this paper, but the greatest life of a regenerated man redeemed by the Blood of

Jesus is yet to come.

"Bibliography"

Backus, William. Telling the Truth to Troubled People. Grand Rapids: Bethany House Publishers, 1985.

Colin M. Turnbull, The Human Cycle. New York: Simon and Schuster, 1983.

Erick Erickson, Childhood and Society. New York. W.W Norton, 1950.

George E. Vaillant, Aging Well: The Study of Adult Development. Boston: Little

Brown and Company, 2002.

Howard Schwartz, Gabriel's Palace: Jewish Mystical Tales. New York: Oxford

University Press, 1993.

Howard Schwartz, Gabriel's Palace: Jewish Mystical Tales. New York: Oxford

University Press, 1993.

James Dobson, The New Strong-Willed Child: The Wild and Woolly Will. Illinois:

Tyndale House Publishing, 2004.

Kanel, Kristi. A Guide to Crisis Intervention. Belmont: Brooks/ Cole Cengage Learning, 2012

Narramore, Clyde. Psychology of Christian Counseling. Pasadena: A Division of Harper

Collins Publishers, 1960.

Martin Hebert, Typical and Atypical Development: From

Conception to Adolescence.

London: Blackwell, 2002.

Olson, Richard P. Ask Anything a Pastoral Theology of Inquiry.
New York: Haworth Pastoral

   Press, 2006.

R. Havinghurst, Developmental Task and Education. New York:
David McKay, 1972.

Richard Jessor, Problem Behavior Theory: Psychosocial
Development, and Adolescent

Problem Drinking. London: British Journal of Addiction, 1987.

Roger Cook, The Tree of Life: Image for the Cosmos. London:
Thames and Hudson, 1988.

Stanislav Grof, Realms of the Human Unconscious: Observation from LSD Research.

London: Souvenir Press, 1994.

Stephen D. Levitt and Stephen J. Dubner, Freakonomics: A Rogue Economist Explores

the Hidden Side of Everything. New York: William Morrows, 2005.

Stephen Jay Gould, Ontogeny and Phylogeny. Cambridge, MA: Belknap Press, 1985.

Wayne, Oates E. Behind the Mask. Louisville: The Westminster Press, 1987.

"Biography"

Tasha Taylor was born in South Florida on September 21, 1982, to her parents Anthony Taylor and Sandra Mitchell. She was a gifted and talented song writer from the age of 8 and sung in the children's choir at, Bethel First Assembly of God. There she was also baptized by Rev. James Peirce at the age of 12 and was filled with the Spirit with the evidence of speaking with other tongues as well. She wrote over 30 songs by the age of 15 and over 50 by the age of 18. As she grew she went through various trials both emotional and physical with the separation of her family at the age of 6, and the remarriage of her mother to Ernest Mitchell. At the age of 7 she was removed from her home church with Rev. Dr. James Peirce and placed into DayStar Ministries where her mother and stepfather founded. Throughout Tasha's life she learned to pray and wait on God to be her vindicator, deliver and way maker. Through Tasha's music God was able to make a way of provision for Tasha during various financial trials in her life. While attending, "DayStar Ministries" Tasha was ordained an "Evangelist" and served for over 20 years in ministry.

Evangelist Tasha Taylor later attended the "School of Prophets" in Miami, FL at the "Rose of Sharon School of Biblical Studies" and also attended the "International Seminary" satellite classes held there. Her first year teacher was, Apostle Dr.

Elizabeth Hairston that has sowed a lot of prophecy in her life. Her second year teacher was none other than her mother, who also help found DayStar Ministries, Pastor Sandra Mitchell. Evangelist Tasha Taylor then attained her Bachelor's Degree from the International Seminary on February 2013. She began Pastoring her own church, "Reaping Time Outreach Global" at the age of 25. She was also newly married to her now ex-husband Michelet Josma. Their marriage lasted 7 years and they had a son named Joshua Josma. Pastor Tasha Taylor began a Christian homeschool in her home and attempted to license 2 daycares in which 1 was cleared. Pastor Tasha's son is currently performing at first grade level at 5 years old and refers to himself as Brilliant. Pastor Tasha Taylor was ordained as a Prophetess by Apostle Michael Hunter founder of Prophetic Minds Ministry in 2009 who also covered her newly established ministry, "Reaping Time Outreach Global." She was later mentored by Apostle Anne Darville of Delray Beach.

\

Pastor Tasha was Ordained a Pastor by the covering Apostles Mitchells' of "DayStar Ministries."

Currently, Pastor Tasha Taylor started a ministry in Marietta, GA for prayer and Bible studies who currently meet in the Intown Suites Hotel located at: 2353 Barrett Creek Parkway, Marietta GA, 30066 on Sundays at 11am. She thrives on Prayer and generates the power to minister from the anointing. Her prayer services are privately held, but those who attend testify of the power of the Holy Ghost in her life, answers to prayer, and the move of the Spirit of God in their lives. She is also the author of five books: "Success that Begins When Asking for Help," "Marriage and Family," "Building Strong Families in Critical Situations," "Human Development," and "Biblical Ethics: Finances."

Made in the USA
Columbia, SC
22 July 2023

20738171R00062